Digging Up The Past
In
Ballyphilip Churchyard

J B McMullan

DEDICATION

In memory of Elsie, Seamus and Gerard

CONTENTS

Acknowledgments   I

1   The Founding Fathers   3

2   The Mariners   15

3   The War   26

4   Police, Pubs and Flying Machines   32

5   The Lightship Men   40

6   The Entertainers   45

7   The Troubles   53

8   Football's Founding Fathers   60

9   Precious Time   69

ACKNOWLEDGMENTS

Reference Material: Souvenir of The Bi-Centenary of St. Patrick's Church Ballyphilip Portaferry, Ballyphilip and Portaferry Parish Registers, National Archives - Census of Ireland 1901 and 1911, irishgenealogy.ie, General Records Office Northern Ireland, Forces War Records, RIC Service Records, Life-Boat Journal, Derry Journal, Down Recorder, Newtownards Chronicle and County Down Observer, Belfast Telegraph. With special thanks to Lawrence Edge.

ALL PROCEEDS IN AID OF CANCER RESEARCH

1 THE FOUNDING FATHERS

St. Patrick's Church Ballyphilip

St. Patrick's Church, Ballyphilip, was established by the Rev. James McTeggart in 1762. Father McTeggart was parish priest of the entire Ards Peninsula from 1754 –1765. He was born in Drumroe, in the parish of Kilclief and was buried in the ancient cemetery of Saul.

The church replaced the old mass house on the same site. Mass houses were usually low, mud-walled sheds, covered with thatch and often having only three sides. The new church ran parallel to the Ballyphilip Road, with the altar at the north gable, and the main door in the south gable. The date-stone built into the wall of the church bears the following inscription:

"All ye good Christians pray for ye benefactors of this Chapel which was built by the Masons Dorrian, and Mr. Murland the carpenter, October 1762."

Rev James Killen

The first parish priest to be buried at Ballyphilip was the Rev. James Killen. He was also the longest serving parish priest from 1843 to 1881. During his long tenure he enlarged the church by building the western wing which is now the central portion of the church. He moved the High Altar from the northern gable to its present location in the eastern side wall of the church and erected three new galleries.

In 1852 he obtained an acre of land from Colonel Andrew Nugent which was used to extend the graveyard and to build the Parochial Schools the following year. This was one building within which boys and girls were educated separately. The date-stone on the front wall of the school bears the inscription: -

"They who instruct many into righteousness shall shine, shine for all eternity. Daniel X11.c3"

When the girls' school was built in 1933 the original school became the Ballyphilip Boys' Primary School and the new school, St. Mary's Girls' School.

Parochial School for boys and girls, 1853

In 1875 a field of three and a half acres on the Ballyfounder Road was leased to Father Killen where he built the first parochial house the following year. In 1879 he erected an altar in honour of St. Patrick on the Gospel side of the High Altar and one on the Epistle side to the Blessed Virgin. The cost came to £500 which was gifted by Misses Murphy of Tara, about £60,000 in today's money.

Original Parochial House, 1876

Situated near the huge black wooden cross in the graveyard, a rather ornate headstone commemorates the long serving Father James Killen:-

"In hope of a happy resurrection
Here lies the body of the
Rev'd James Killen
Who for thirty eight years
Previous to his death
Had been P.P. of Portaferry
He was born the 17th November 1806
Died on the 6th February 1881,
In the fiftieth year
Of his priesthood
RIP"

Father Killen was succeeded by his brother Richard who became parish priest on 10th February 1881. He had been appointed parish priest of Coleraine on 20th April 1848, and while there he erected the chancel of the Church of Coleraine. He then moved to Bright in 1856, where he was parish priest for 26 years, before succeeding his brother as parish priest of Ballyphilip. He died in 1898, aged 84, and was buried in the same grave as his brother. Consequently, the Rev. Killens served as Portaferry parish priests for a continuous period of more than half a century.

Father Hugh Magorrian

Father Magorrian was born in Ballykinlar on 2nd April 1845. He was appointed curate of Newtownards on 1st August 1869 and parish priest of Drummaul in September 1884. Fifteen years later he became parish priest of Ballyphilip on 1st January 1899. In July of that year he obtained a site at Shore Street from Colonel Nugent and built St Patrick's Parochial Hall the following year.

St Patrick's Parochial Hall, 1900

Very Rev. James Canon Kennedy

Father Magorrian died on 5th May 1912, his headstone bears the following inscription:

Pray For
The Very Rev. Hugh Magorrian, P.P. V.F.
Born April 2nd 1845
Ordained July 1869
Appointed Parish Priest
Portaferry, Jan. 1st 1899
Died May 5th 1912
Grant Eternal Rest O' Lord

He was succeeded by the Very Rev. G. Crolly from 1912 to 1915. During his three years as parish priest he built the bell tower and new sacristy. The tower was completed in December 1914 and, having made a significant contribution to the parish in a short time, Father Crolly went on to be parish priest of St Mathews in Belfast the following year.

Father Kennedy was born in Ardglass on 8th October 1852 and was parish priest of Ballyphilip from 1916 to 1928. On 19th September 1916 he purchased the house at 42 Shore Street as a residence for the curate. This house was in close proximity to the Parochial Hall which contained a small oratory. On Holy Days and other occasions an early mass, known as the 'workers mass,' would be celebrated in the oratory. This early mass allowed workers to attend mass before heading off to work. At such times the proximity of the house to the oratory would have been of considerable convenience to the parish curate.

The curate's house, Shore Street.

Very Rev. Patrick McKillop

On 17th August 1917 Father Kennedy purchased a field on the Windmill Hill for a new cemetery, and on 7th June 1921, he purchased the field opposite the parochial house, known as the 'tennis court' field because of its shape and flatness. The marble High Altar in the church was erected by Father Kennedy in September 1923 and he was later appointed Canon of the Diocese. Canon Kennedy died on 7th May 1929. His headstone is dedicated to Christ the King with the inscription: -

Father McKillop was born in Loughgiel on 16th October 1869 and was parish priest at Ballyphilip from 1929 to 1945. On 18th October 1930 he purchased a three-acre field known as the Tullyboard Field, at the cost of £150, to build a new girls' school. The school was opened on 13th April 1933 and cost £6,400, half of which was received from the Ministry of Education.

St Mary's Girls' School, 1933

Very Rev. George Watson

He had also bought a two-acre field known as 'Wilson's Field' which allowed the graveyard to be extended by half an acre in 1935. An extra classroom was added to Ballyphilip Boys' School in 1935 at a cost of £625. In 1939, a gift from an anonymous donor, funded a new bell weighing 16½ cwt which was installed in the church tower. Father McKillop died on 23rd November 1945 having served as parish priest for 16 years.

Father Watson was born at Slanes in Ballygalget and was parish priest at Ballyphilip from 1946 to 1960. He was a progressive priest who got things done and his legacy is evident in the parish to the present day. One of his first duties was to repair the roof of St Patrick's Church which had fallen into such a state of disrepair that it was in danger of falling down. The work included new steel girders to support the roof, re-roofing of the church, re-plastering ceilings and walls, new heating and electric light systems. It was completed in 1949 at a cost of £9,500.

In 1947 he purchased a field of 6½ acres from James McCarthy for a parochial playing field at a cost of £160. Most of the work was carried out by the men of the parish and it was completed in July 1949 at a cost of £2,000. At the time it was considered to be one of the finest parochial parks in Ireland.

The opening of the Parochial Park, 1949

In April 1951 the Boys' Primary School was re-roofed and in 1952 two new classrooms and toilets were added at a cost of £14,500. To commemorate the Marian Year of 1954 a Lourdes Grotto was erected and opened by the Most Rev. Dr. Mageenan on 31 May 1955. Most of the work again was carried out by the men of the parish. In 1955 two fields at the top of High Street were purchased as a site for a new Intermediate School. Work began on 14th January 1957 and the new St Columba's Intermediate School was completed and opened on 6th January 1959 with twelve teachers. The total cost of the school was £96,110, the Ministry of Education granted £62,472 and the rest was paid by the three main parishes using the school, Portaferry, Kircubbin and Ballygalget.

John Merrick

Father Watson and John Merrick admiring the new school

The first principal of the school was John Merrick MA, who was born in Scotland to Irish parents, his father being from Sligo. He arrived in Northern Ireland shortly after the war from his Clarkston, Glasgow, home to take up a post in St Patrick's High School in Downpatrick. He was principal of Ballycruttle School before taking up his appointment at St Columba's Portaferry. John Merrick had the drive and determination to take forward the new school. By 1973 the school was providing pupils with the opportunity to take both 'O' Levels and 'A' Levels, thus enabling many to seamlessly progress from education in Portaferry through to university. John Merrick died in his late fifties on 11th May 1976.

Also, in 1957 work began on the building of a new parochial house, which was completed and occupied by Father Watson on 11 July 1958. The Park, School and Parochial House are all still functional to the present day and stand as a testament to the work of Father Watson who died on 8th November 1960.

The new parochial house, 1958

Very Rev. Patrick McAlea

Father McAlea was born in Crunglass near Ardglass 1901 and was parish priest at Ballyphilip from 1960 to 1965. He had previously been in St Mary's in Belfast, where he had acted as chaplain to the Hungarian refugees who had fled from Russian tyranny in 1956. After the revolution he was invited to spend a holiday in Hungary by some of the refugees he had befriended.

During his time as parish priest preparatory work began on the building of a new oratory in The Square. He purchased two shops in The Square, a house in Church Street and nearby local residents donated part of their back gardens for the site.

Architects McLean and Forte were appointed and an innovative design was agreed upon. The ceiling of the church resembled the hull of a boat in keeping with Portaferry's maritime tradition. There was a courtyard in front of the church with a free-standing tower fitted with a bell that was once used at St Patrick's. With the planning work done the completion of the work was taken forward by father McAlea's successor, the Very Rev. David Morgan. Father McAlea died on 2 December 1972.

Very Rev. David Morgan

Father Morgan was born in 1905 and was parish priest at Ballyphilip from 1965 to 1985, the second longest serving parish priest. His legacy includes the building of the new oratory and the renovation of St Cooey's Wells.

Father Morgan choose St Cooey as the patron saint for the new oratory and building work got underway in Christmas week 1966. Foundation stones were brought from the 7th century Temple Cooey Church and two ancient stones from that location now stand outside the oratory. St Cooey's oratory was completed and opened on 29th June 1969 by Bishop William Philbin. Father McAlea also attended, having the satisfaction of seeing the work he had started, brought to its conclusion in a very fine building.

The site of the ancient church of St Cooey, deep in the Portaferry country-side, off the Ballyquintin Road also contained Holy Wells. By the 1970s, however, they had become overgrown, were almost inaccessible and in danger of being lost to the parish. On 2nd June 1976, Father Morgan called a meeting of parishioners and a plan was drawn up to renovate the site.

John Johnston donated the land for a new concrete access road with, sloping path and steps, down to the wells. The back-breaking work was carried out by the men of the parish.

Father Morgan with the St. Cooey's workers

It was officially opened on 2nd July 1978 with a mass at the new altar that had been constructed on the site of the old church. Over one thousand people attended and an annual mass has been well attended every year since. Father Morgan died on 17th December 1989.

For more than 250 years the 'founding fathers' have worked closely with their parishioners in an effort to improve the parish for the people of Portaferry. They have provided places for worship, education, sport and entertainment. Each in their turn and time, has sought to add to and build on what has gone before, as a legacy for the next generation. And each in their turn, has found their final resting place in Ballyphilip churchyard, where they are now commemorated.

Altar at St Cooey's Wells

2 THE MARINERS

Captain Hugh Crangle

"I must go down to the seas again, for the call of the running tide

Is a wild call and a clear call that cannot be denied;"

Sea Fever – John Masefield.

John Masefield's poem, Sea Fever, captures how the call of the sea draws men to the sea-faring way of life. It is a call that was answered by many men from Portaferry. In the mid-nineteenth century Portaferry was a busy port full of master mariners, shipbuilders, shipowners, rope-makers, ships' chandlers, ferry-men and fishermen. It was a call that was certainly answered by the Crangles.

On the two headstones above there are no

fewer than four sea-captains commemorated: Captain Rowland Crangle who died on 18 May 1868, his sons Captain Edward Henry who died in California and Captain William John Crangle. In the grave with the white marble headstone there is also a Captain Patrick Crangle who died on 29 October 1912. And still there is a Captain unaccounted for, namely, Captain Hugh Crangle.

Captain Hugh Crangle was captain and part-owner of the Andrew Nugent. This was a brig cargo vessel with two masts and a burthen of 164 tons. It was launched from the Thomas Gelson shipyard in 1826, in a scene that was vividly recalled at the time by Presbyterian minister, the Rev. John Orr:-

"Notice having been given that a very beautiful vessel of 300 tons would be launched from the shipyard of Mr. Thomas Gelston at one o'clock, the fineness of the day, and the novelty of the scene collected together an immense assemblage. On the signal being given the 'Andrew Nugent' glided majestically into her native element amidst the cheers of thousands of spectators.

I never saw so many people in Portaferry on any occasion. In the evening about 30 gentlemen sat down to dinner in Mr. Gelston's. I had the honour of being one of the party."

With dinner over the Andrew Nugent was soon put to work, operating out of Sligo, for the traders Messrs Scott and Partickson. Records show Captain Crangle leaving Sligo on 24th June 1828 and arriving at the Port of Quebec on 5th August 1828 with 80 "settlers". The same journey was undertaken from Sligo on 21 May 1834 landing at Grosse Isle, Quebec on 3rd July 1834 with 194 passengers. It was a journey that Captain Crangle and the Andrew Nugent would become very familiar with, as they continued with this route to North America for up to a decade, until the fateful Night of the Big Wind in 1839.

The Night of the Big Wind on 6th January 1839 blew the sails off Portaferry Windmill, damaged houses and buildings in the town, tore boats from their moorings and swept them up onto the shore. It was not a night to be out and far less a night to be out on the high seas in the Andrew Nugent, as was Captain Crangle's fate.

According to reports there was an eerie calm before the storm on 6th January. Captain Crangle had set sail on calm seas with a cargo of butter, bacon and other general provisions bound for London. With his vast experience of crossing the Atlantic, back and forward to Canada, the trip should really have been something of a leisure cruise. However, by 6 o'clock the wind began to rise, by bed-time it had increased to a gale and by mid-night it had become a hurricane. For the next 6 hours the storm raged relentlessly.

With the storm whipping up mountainous seas the Andrew Nugent ran into difficulty and Captain Crangle made for anchorage at Arran Roads, off the Donegall coast, on the evening of the 7th. The islanders around the

Rosses in Donegall, aware of the ship's difficulty, lit beacons on the shore-line to direct Captain Crangle on a safe course to the anchorage between Arranmore and Rutland. This seemed to work and the Andrew Nugent tacked and sailed across North Bay until she was near the shore off Pollawaddy in Arranmore. A small boat headed out to the stricken ship from Rutland Harbour but the heavy seas made it impossible for it to come alongside. Somehow, the Pilot Tom O'Donnel, managed to get on board but due to worsening conditions the small boat had to return to harbour, leaving Tom O'Donnel to assist Captain Crangle.

With their combined skills they managed to bring the Andrew Nugent to the anchorage at Arran Roads where they dropped anchor for the night. It is thought at this stage that many of the 14 crew members had already been swept overboard. The Andrew Nugent seemed now to be riding out the storm safely but before dawn on the 8th January the wind changed and tore the ship from its moorings and onto the rocks. The ship struck Duck Island and was swept southwards coming to rest west of Rutland. The ship was wrecked and all on board perished.

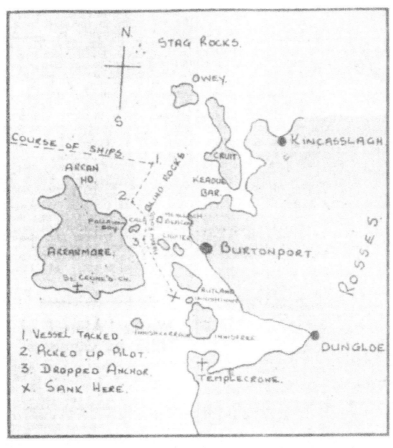

Map showing Rosses course of the "Andrew Nugent."

The shores off the Rosses were strewn with wreckage for weeks to come and while the authorities did their best to salvage the cargo, recovering 992 casks of butter and 82 of bacon, the locals accumulated a huge amount of butter for themselves. On the morning after the shipwreck, a rock in Dungloe Bay that is only covered at high tide, was found with a cask of butter on top, it was subsequently named Carraig an Ime – the Butter Rock.

Captain Crangle's body was washed up on the beach at Innishinna, a little island north of Innisfree in Dungloe Bay. His remains were left overnight in St Peter's Church, Dungloe where candles were lit and locals came to pay their respects to a brave sea Captain. He was buried in the near-by Templecrone cemetery.

Templecrone Cemetery, Dungloe

John Scott, of Messrs. Scott and Partickson, on hearing of the disaster made his way to Rutland and in a letter dated 15th January 1839, reported:-

"I saw the spot on which the body of poor Crangle was found; he had on only his trousers, vest, shirt, and stockings, no shoes or jacket, but his cap on his head. He could not have been dead when the vessel was wrecked. He has been the most respectably interred in the graveyard of Templecrone by Priest Mac Devitt—the captains of the vessels here (Rutland), the coast-guard, etc., attending. It was impossible to procure a leaden coffin here, otherwise I would have had the remains conveyed to Sligo."

And so, the body of Captain Hugh Crangle from Tara, Portaferry, is accounted for not in Ballyphilip Churchyard alongside the other Captain Crangles, but many miles from home in Templecrone Cemetery, Dungloe, County Donegall.

James McCausland

The tallest headstone in the graveyard is a 20ft., grey granite, Celtic Cross, erected by Susan McCausland in memory of her husband James who died on 18 July 1915, aged 65. On the side panel of the headstone there is also the intriguing inscription 'Also Charles McCausland of New Orleans died 1898 aged 38 years.'

James McCausland was an internationally known salvage contractor and was called upon to raise sunken ships in many parts of the world. His skills had been honed closer to home with the many outcrops of rock around the County Down coast being, particularly, hazardous to shipping at the time. Numerous accounts in local papers report incidents from Cloghy Rocks, Angus Rock (the Rockin' Goose), Pladdy Lug, Ballyquintin Point, Kearney Point, South Rock and North Rocks, running from Strangford to Cloughey.

In 1870 Strangford Harbourmaster, William Russel, estimated from his records, that between 1833 and 1867 seventy vessels had been wrecked or badly damaged in the area, with the loss of forty-three lives. It was a dangerous time for shipping and a busy time for a salvage operator. James McCausland's salvage business at Ballyhenry Bay and the Saltpans, consequently, provided much needed local employment at this time.

As well as saving ships his business by its nature, at times, also involved saving lives. The most famous being in relation to the French barque the Cannebiere that got into difficulties in Dundrum Bay in 1905.

The Cannebiere

The Cannebiere was a large steel-built French barque of upwards of 3,000 tons. It had set sail from the Clyde on 7th March 1905 with 1,500 tons of coal bound for the French colony, New Caledonia. With a storm brewing Captain Lefeuvre took shelter for a time before heading out into the Irish Sea. But when he did the storm worsened to a Force 10 and the Cannebiere lost all sails and was soon without power or steerage. The ship was spotted on 15th March off Annalong and the Newcastle Life-Boat was alerted.

Due to the lack of a tide the life-boat, Farnley, could not launch immediately. Also, in Newcastle harbour was James McCausland's new ship. He had purchased a steam paddle-tug called the Flying Serpent, only a month before, which was renamed the Flying Irishman. At four o'clock in the afternoon the tug got up steam and caught the tide towards the stricken vessel, now in Dundrum Bay. The Newcastle Life-Boat, Farnley, was also underway under the command of Coxswain Superintendent, James Foland.

The Jim McCausland

Within distance of the stricken vessel the Farnley lost her anchor and was cast ashore at Ballykinler. Things were becoming desperate aboard the Cannebiere, with the heavy cargo of coal, she was low in the water and the decks were awash. In a last desperate attempt to save their lives the crew had taken to the rigging.

James McCausland's tug, under the command of his son John, could not have arrived soon enough when she managed to anchor in the lee of the Cannebiere. Two seamen, Lawrence Ivers and Joe McGuigan, whose bravery cannot be overstated, took to the rowing boat and got close enough to the Cannebiere to rescue nine of the crew. By this time the Farnley had returned and was able to save ten more of the crew. The only casualty was the ship's cook who, unfortunately, had fallen from the rigging and was washed overboard.

In 1906, John McCausland, James Foland, Lawrence Ivers and Joe McGuigan were presented with diplomas and gold medals, by the Lord Mayor of Belfast, Sir Danial Dixon, on behalf of the French Government.

James McCausland managed to re-float the Cannebiere to literally fight another day. Unfortunately, she met her end when she was sunk by the German U-boat, Otto Steinbrinck, on 24 October 1916, in the Atlantic Ocean, 20 miles SSW off Bishop Rock, Isle of Scilly.

The following obituary to James McCausland appeared in the Down Recorder on 24th July 1915:-

"A man of action, known far beyond the limits of County Down, in the person of Mr. James McCausland, died on Sunday after a lengthened illness at his residence, Westgate, Portaferry, at the age of 65. Mr McCausland achieved considerable fame in the salvage of wrecks. In many instances, in different parts of the world, he succeeded in raising sunken vessels where other firms had failed. It is remembered how when the French barque, Cannebiere, foundered in Dundrum Bay of a tempestuous night one of his steamers ran down and took off the crew.

To his enterprise the labouring population of Portaferry were indebted for employment one winter in the scrapping of three condemned war vessels which he purchased from the Admiralty. His probity and large-heartedness won him at once respect and esteem. Certainly he will be much missed. On Tuesday his remains were laid to rest in Ballyphilip graveyard. He is survived by a widow and two sons."

In this instance 'a man of action' perhaps appropriately describes the adventurous life of James McCausland.

Henry Hutton

This headstone was erected by Henry Hutton in memory of his wife Eliza who died on 24th May 1904 aged 40 years and also his daughter Eliza who died, less than three months later, on 2nd August 1904, aged 19 years.

While his son Thomas (Tommy) was interred in 1980, aged 83 years, there is no reference on the headstone to Henry's interment. Henry Hutton and his eldest son John were boatmen and provided a ferry service between Portaferry and Strangford.

With the distance between Portaferry and Strangford, across the lough, being less than a mile and almost 50 miles by road around the peninsula, it was inevitable that a ferry service would grow up between these two points.

There are records that a ferry service of some description existed since around 1180. In 1611 King James I granted land on either side of the lough to Peirce Tumolton in order to maintain and crew a ferry boat. And for more than 400 years a ferry service has been provided without a break.

In 1835 a group of local people formed the 'Portaferry and Strangford Steamboat Company' and commissioned the building of the 'Lady of the Lake', which was the first steamboat in Ireland. It was more than 30 years later that Belfast got its first steamboat in 1872. The 'Lady of the Lake's' maiden voyage was on 18th June 1836 just two hours after arriving in Portaferry. The venture, however, was not a commercial success and the ferry was sold in 1839.

The Lady of the Lake, 1836

In 1946 two converted World War II landing craft were introduced, capable of carrying 36 passengers and 2 motor cars, and often cited as the first car-ferry service on the lough. Although as the photo below shows some of the wooden sailing boats precariously tried to keep pace with the changing times.

In 1947 one of the landing craft capsized with the loss of one life and all animals on board which led to the service being discontinued. It was not until 1969 that the present car ferry service was introduced.

An Early Car Ferry

For the vast majority of the 400 years, that there has continuously been a ferry service, it has been provided by local families in relatively small wooden boats. They carried passengers and cargo and at times livestock. It was from one such vessel, named the "Lizzie," that Henry Hutton and his son John plied their trade until a tragic accident on 11th April 1913, which was reported in the Down Recorder the following day:-

STRANGFORD LOUGH DISASTER

THREE PERSONS DROWNED

"Last night intelligence reached us of a shocking accident in Strangford Lough, off Oldcourt, whereby three Portaferry residents, Henry Hutton, ferry-man, his son, John, aged about 17 years, and Mrs Mason, lost their lives.

It appears that Mr. John McCausland, son of Mr. James McCausland, salvage contractor, Portaferry, with his wife and his sister-in-law, Mrs. Mason, visited an ailing relative in Downpatrick yesterday. Returning to Strangford in the evening, they set out for Portaferry at five o'clock in a ferryboat manned by the Huttons, father and son.

There was a strong ebb tide, with a stiff north-west wind. As the boat, under sail, was standing up past Oldcourt, at a point about 200 yards from the Slip, she was struck by a heavy squall, and capsized. The five occupants were flung into the water. It was with consternation that the accident was observed from the Strangford shore. But

prompt measures were taken.

Several boats were manned and put off. Dick Farrow, Dr. MacLaughlin's yachtsman, in a boat that was first to reach the scene, succeeded in saving Mr. McCausland and his wife. Powerful swimmer though Mr. McCausland is, he was nearly exhausted in the struggle to support his wife. Meantime, James Quayle, in his motor boat, picked up Mrs Mason, in an apparently lifeless condition. Of the Huttons, however, there was no sign. They had been swept away by the strong current.

Mr. and Mrs. McCausland were taken ashore, and received every attention. Unhappily, there was no hope for Mrs Mason, though every effort was made to restore animation, first by members of the rescue party, and then by Drs McDonald and Smyth, who had come across from Portaferry.

When the dire news became known on both sides of the Lough it created a painful impression. Portaferry has been plunged into mourning, and deep sympathy is felt with those who have been so swiftly and cruelly bereaved.

Harry Hutton was an experienced boatman, as ready to undertake a trip to the Isle of Man as to cross the ferry. It is only a few short weeks ago, on the 13th ult., to be exact, that he helped to succour a boat's crew in danger of being swamped in one of the whirlpools of the Lough. His son was equally handy and courageous.

Widely known as a skilled yachtsman, and even better known for his salvage work on different parts of the coast of the United Kingdom, Mr. McCausland has on several occasions shown signal heroism. One of his achievements was the part he played in the rescue on a tempestuous night of the crew of the Cannebiere, wrecked in Dundrum Bay some years ago, for which act of bravery the French Government rewarded him with a gold medal.

Yesterday's calamity is another reminder of the treacherous nature of the windswept, eddying currents of the lower reaches of the Lough, which has so often taken toll of human life."

Sadly, Henry Hutton died aged 48 and his son John died aged 19 when their boat the "Lizzie" capsized on 11th April 1913. John's body was never recovered but on 2 June 1913 Henry's body was found floating beside Ballydorn Quay and was interred in the family grave at Ballyphilip following a very large funeral.

Young Tommy, by the age of 16 had lost both his parents and two siblings. Despite the dire warning in the Down Recorder of the treacherous nature of the lough, Tommy followed in his father's footsteps. In January 1914 he took delivery of a new ferryboat, Star of the Sea, fitted with a Kelvin motor engine as well as sails and with a hood to protect passengers from spray and rain. It was built in Belfast to Board of Trade standards and was the largest and most powerful boat on the Lough.

He was boatman/ferryman for many decades and one of the most experienced men on the lough. He died on 6th February 1980 aged 83, and despite his passing, his spirit still seems to be at the shore-front where he spent all his life.

3. THE WAR

Prior to the outbreak of the First World War tensions in the country and in Portaferry were running high due to the proposed Home Rule Act. Some young men in the town had joined the Irish National Volunteers, Portaferry Company, 1st Battalion, East Down Regiment, which supported Home Rule, while others, who opposed it, had joined the Ulster Volunteer Force. With the outbreak of war these local differences were put aside and they joined forces to fight a common foe.

Many of these young men who went off to war, never returned to see Portaferry ever again, and are buried in a foreign field many miles from home. It is estimated that at least

53 men with connections to Portaferry died in the First World War. Among these were John Delaney, Edward McMullan and Dr Hugh McNally from The Shore, Hugh Dorrian and James Fitzsimmons from Knocknagow, Samuel Orr and John Croskery from Church Street, Bernard Kerr from High Street and Thomas Emerson from Ballyphilip.

Regiments of the British Army to support the war effort, with the view, that this was more likely to lead to the implementation of Home Rule when the war was over. Thomas answered the call and joined the "B" Company, 6th Battalion of the Royal Irish Regiment.

Portaferry Company of the Irish National Volunteers

Thomas Guiney was typical of many of these young men. He was the son of Thomas and Eliza Jane Guiney with three sisters, Elizabeth, Mary Catherine and Annie. In 1911 he was working as a labourer, and living with his mother and Mary Catherine, at 28 Big Back Lane, his father having died the previous year, on 10 September 1910.

Before the war Thomas had joined the Irish National Volunteers in Portaferry. When war broke out, John Redmond, the leader of the volunteers, called on volunteers to join Irish

The Royal Irish Regiment was part of the 16th Irish Division which saw action at the Somme in France. The battle of the Somme started on the 1st July 1916 and continued to 18th November 1916. It was the first great offensive of World War One and one of the bloodiest battles in history. On the first day alone 100,000 allied troops went over the top, resulting in 60,000 casualties and 20,000 deaths. In total, there were over one million casualties and over 300,000 men were killed or declared missing.

The 16th Irish Division was involved in the attacks on Guillemont and Ginchy, two strategic positions, as these villages were on hilltops overlooking the British and French lines and occupied by the Germans. The 8th Munsters and Thomas's 6th Battalion led the attack on Ginchy on 9th September 1916. They were met with fierce resistance and of the 1,328 men involved in the attack, 448, a third became casualties. At the end of the battle Ginchy had all but been wiped off the face of the earth. One private at the time commented: "There was no village there now, only a hole in the ground."

Private Thomas Guiney

Thomas is commemorated on the family grave headstone in Ballyphilip with the inscription: "Killed In France 9th September 1916." He is, however, buried in Delville Wood Cemetery, Longueval in France. Delville Wood, was also known as Devil's Wood, as it was the scene of some of the heaviest fighting during the Battle of the Somme, to the extent that at the end of the fighting, not a single tree in the wood was left standing.

Delville Wood Cemetery is the third largest cemetery in the Somme battlefield area and the final resting place of over 5,500 servicemen, of whom 3,500 remain unidentified. Initially, Thomas was buried in a smaller cemetery closer to the battlefields and identified by a simple wooden cross. The bodies in these cemeteries were exhumed and re-buried in Delville Wood Cemetery where the Commonwealth War Graves Commission could ensure proper commemoration and maintenance of the graves. His headstone bears the inscription: -

"O SCARED HEART OF JESUS HAVE MERCY ON HIS SOUL R.I.P."

John Joseph Sheals

John Joseph Sheals lived only a few doors from Thomas Guiney in Big Back Lane. He was born on 24th June 1876, son of Thomas and Sarah Sheals (nee Smyth) who were married at Ballyphillip on 10th January 1875. His father, Thomas, worked as a boatman.

In 1901 he was living at 30 Big Back Lane with his father, aged 83, and his aunt Alice McNamara, aged 59, his mother having died on 19th March 1893, aged 60 years.

At that point he was already serving in the Royal Navy. His father stated on his Census return that he was "supported by his son in Royal Navy." By 1911, however, at the age of 35, John Joseph had left the Royal Navy and gives his occupation as "Seaman Naval Pensioner." With the outbreak of war he was re-employed by the Navy as a Petty Officer First Class.

He was assigned to 'HMS Pembroke', Chatham. This was a naval training establishment in Gillingham, near London, which provided training and accommodation for men waiting to be appointed to ships. It is likely that John Joseph, with his previous naval experience, was employed in a training capacity for new recruits, rather than on board a war-going ship.

On Saturday 27th January 1917, while on a period of leave and preparing to return to Portaferry, he met with a fatal accident, which was reported in the Newtownards Chronicle and County Down Observer on 3rd February 1917: -

Portaferry Naval Officer's Death

" An inquest was held on Wednesday at St. Pancras, London, by Mr. P. Byrne, on John Joseph Shiels, 42, whose home was Meeting-house Lane, Portaferry. Evidence given showed that the deceased was a first-class petty officer in the Royal Navy. On January 19th he left his ship on leave for the purpose of visiting his home in Ireland. On Saturday, while walking along Euston Road, he was seen to stagger and fall, striking his head on the pavement. He was removed to University College Hospital, where he became unconscious soon after his admission, and died in a couple of hours. Dr. Hickson stated that there was fracture of the skull, and a piece of the broken bone had lacerated the brain. Death was due to effusion of blood on the brain produced through the deceased having struck his head on the ground. The jury returned a verdict of accidental death."

The Royal Navy arranged for the body to be brought back to Portaferry, where John Joseph was laid to rest at Ballyphilip with full naval honours. The inscription on his headstone reads: -

IHS

In memory of John Joseph Sheals died 27th January 1917 aged 42 years

His mother Sarah Sheals died 19 March 1893 aged 60 years

Also his aunt Alice McNamara, died 16 April 1927 aged 83 years

RIP

John Hogan

John Hogan has the unfortunate distinction of being the first man from Portaferry to die in the war, without a shot being fired and without leaving home, unlike many of his fallen comrades, he was buried in Ballyphilip Churchyard. John was born on 9th January1878 in Garrycahara, Fermoy, County Cork son of John and Ellen Hogan. John Married Catherine O'Connell on 27th July 1897 in Ballynoe Roman Catholic Church, Fermoy.

They subsequently moved to Portaferry where they lived at Derry Cottages.

As part of coastal defences look-out posts and signal stations were established at strategic points along the coast. An example of a World War II look-out post can still be seen at Ballyquintin Point.

World War II Look-Out Post, Ballyquintin

Before the war John worked as a labourer and seaman and immediately joined the Royal Naval Coast Guard when war was declared. He was employed as 'leading-boatman' at Tara War Signal Station, where he monitored shipping.

He met with a fatal accident, at Ballyfounder, similar to that of his naval comrade John Joseph Sheals, which resulted in a fractured skull and he died on 20th September 1914, aged 35. Catherine was pregnant at the time and four months later gave birth to Kathleen Elizabeth on 10 January 1915. Kathleen is also buried in this grave when she died aged 29 on 23rd February 1944. Her brother William, also interred, had died 10 years earlier at the age of 28 on 8th July 1928. Catherine herself died on 13th February 1937, aged 63 years.

4 POLICE, PUBS AND FLYING MACHINES

John Knox

This rather distinctive, polished marble headstone, was erected by John Knox Hinds in 'loving and grateful remembrance' of John Knox. The inscription indicates that John Knox was a head constable in the Royal Irish Constabulary. A middle-ranking officer at the time. This force was founded in 1822 as the Irish Constabulary with the pre-fix "Royal" being conferred by Queen Victoria in 1867. It was a predominantly Catholic force although there were fewer Catholics in the higher ranks. With the partition of Ireland in 1921, the force was disbanded in 1922, to be replaced by the Garda Siochana in the South and the Royal Ulster Constabulary in the North.

John was a native of Fermanagh and joined the force on 13th May 1844, his age is recorded as 24 when, in fact, he was only 18. The minimum age for entry to the force was 19 but lowered to 18 for sons of policemen. As John's father was a farmer this does not explain the age discrepancy and may simply be an error.

Recruits could not serve in their own native county and John Knox served in Cavan, Armagh, Down, Clare and finally Belfast from 21st December 1870. It was perhaps while serving in Down that John met Maria Hinds (nee Glass) in Portaferry, a widow who ran a grocer's shop.

An intended wife of a RIC officer had to be vetted by senior officers before getting married. If permission was granted the couple had to transfer to a county where neither had relatives. It was also a condition that members needed to have, at least, seven years' service before getting married.

John had been in the force 30 years when he married Maria at Ballyphilip on 10th May 1874, he was aged 48 and Maria 38. Despite being ten years younger Maria pre-deceased John and died on 6th February 1895, aged 58 years. She was buried in the same grave as her first husband John Hinds who had died nearly 30 years earlier, aged 45. The inscription on

that gravestone also refers to "children who died young" which perhaps influenced Maria's choice of burial place.

John Hinds and Maria Knox

In the 1901 Census John Knox describes himself as a RIC pensioner, a widower and living at 85 High Street with his grandson John Knox Hinds, a scholar, and servant Mary Ann Donnan. He died later that year aged 75.

John Knox Hinds

John Knox Hinds was, in fact, the step-grandson of John Knox. Maria Glass's first marriage was to John Hinds publican/shopkeeper (spirit-grocer), on 2nd June 1857. Their first son, also John, was born on 6th June 1858. He carried on the family business and married Mary Bryce on 24th September 1879. Mary's father was Edward Bryce who in 1860 had leased the corner property at the shore front, now the Portaferry Hotel, and ran a spirit-grocers' there for the next two decades. John and Mary's first son, born on 12th November 1880, was the said John Knox Hinds.

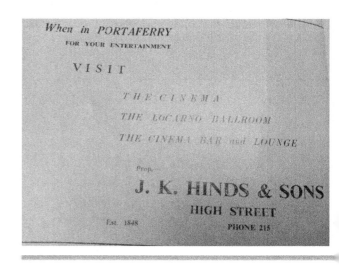

As the above advert from the 1960s shows, the business had been established in his grandfather's day, in 1848. John Knox had expanded it to include the Cinema and the Locarno Ballroom both of which attracted large crowds in their heyday. John Knox Hinds died on 5th March 1943, aged 63, having made more than a significant contribution to life in Portaferry.

John Knox Hinds

At the time of the 1901 Census John Knox Hinds was age 20 and still a scholar. Three years later he married Agnes Gilmore from Kircubbin, on 15th June 1904, at that point, he had been living in Belfast and working as an engineer. He returned to Portaferry and by 1911 he had four children, and in keeping with his family tradition, had set up as a publican at 32 High Street. A location where Hinds' Bar flourished for many years.

'Doc John' Hinds

This headstone was erected in memory of another John Hinds from the same Hinds family and known as 'Doc John'. John was a consultant anesthetist at Craigavon Area Hospital and a member of a team known as 'The Flying Doctors'.

This was an elite team of motor-cycling medics who provided medical cover at motor-cycling events. Their role was to ride behind the racers and provide a rapid response, often within seconds, whenever an incident occurred. By so doing, 'Doc John' had been involved in saving many lives.

One such person was Violet McAfee who had been caught up in a three-bike crash at the NW200 in May 2015. Ms McAfee was in a garden watching the race when the accident happened and she sustained serious head and leg injuries. 'Doc John' was on the scene almost immediately and was able to stabilize her condition until the Coastguard Helicopter arrived and took her to the Royal Victoria Hospital.

John had been an avid campaigner for a Northern Ireland Air Ambulance for many years. The use of the Coastguard Helicopter to get a person to the right hospital quickly, which greatly assisted Violet's recovery, gave him the platform to pursue this with added vigour, and with the clear evidence of its life-saving benefits.

A couple of months after this event on 3rd July 2015 'Doc John' was travelling behind the riders at the opening practice lap of the Skerries 100 when he lost control of his bike and crashed into a wall. He was taken to Beaumont Hospital in Dublin but died the next day from traumatic injuries. Bikers accompanied the cortege, on its way back to Portaferry, detouring for a tribute lap of the Tandragee 100 in his honour.

His shock death brought renewed impetus for an air ambulance for Northern Ireland and his partner Dr. Janet Acheson took up the campaign. Eight months after his death, on what would have been 'Doc John's' 36th birthday, on 21st March 2016, it was announced that funding would be made available for an air ambulance.

It went into service in July 2017 and in its first year responded to more than 500 incidents. On 9th September 2019 it had reached the emergency number of 999 call-outs.

'Doc John' Hinds died aged 35 but others are alive today because of his work. The Air Ambulance Northern Ireland is his lasting legacy that continues to save lives.

Edward Bryce

As previously mentioned in this Chapter, Edward Bryce had acquired the lease for the property at the shore-front on the corner of the Strand and Castle Street around 1860. The original terms of the lease did not permit the premises to be used as a 'tavern or public house for the sale of spirituous liquors.' Eventually, he did obtain his landlord, Andrew Nugent's, permission to open a spirit-grocers' which he ran for nearly two decades.

It was really a prime site as there was still a lot of commercial and shipping activity in the area, which would have provided more than a good passing trade. Only a few years earlier it would have been possible to board a ship right outside the premises bound for America or Canada.

Running a spirit-grocers' and the good sea-air obviously had a conducive effect on Edward's

health as he was 93 years of age when he died, on 3rd April 1909. By contrast, his son Hugh, also buried in this grave died at only age 5. Edward's death was registered by his grandson, John Knox Hinds.

Henry and Hannah McGrath

Edward Bryce had sold his lease to Henry McGrath in 1880 and for the next 50 years it was known as 'McGrath's of the Quay.' Henry was baptized at Ballyphilip on 8th November 1852 and married Hannah Lennon there on 12th November 1885. In the 1901 Census he states his occupation as "auctioneer and publican", he is employing three servants, one Margaret Mageean, is employed as a barmaid as well as domestic servant.

A report in the Down Recorder on 2nd January 1909 about an incident at the quay makes specific reference to Mr. and Mrs. McGrath: -

" About 11p.m. on the 26th ult. Sergeant Reynolds and Constable Ledwith heard shouts from the direction of the dock. On hastening thither, they found that Peter Grant, engineer on the tug, Susan McCausland, had fallen into the dock between the little quay and the S.S. Duke of Edinburgh, which was lying alongside, and that a companion, Andrew Rogan, had descended into the dock to try to rescue him. The night was pitch dark nor was the lamp at the end of the dock lighted. Until he obtained a lifebelt and rope, Sergeant Reynolds rolled his cape, and Rogan gave one end to Grant and Constable Ledwith held the other end above. When the rope was brought, Rogan tied it round Grant, and the police hauled him safely to the quay, the process being repeated in Rogan's turn. Meanwhile, Mr. H. McGrath and some members of his family arrived and rendered valuable assistance. It was found that John Maxwell, a diver in Mr. McCausland's employment, had his foot jammed between a beam of wood and the quay, from which dangerous position he was duly extricated. Mr. and Mrs. McGrath extended generous hospitality to rescued and rescuers."

With perhaps less excitement the lease was bought by William Lyons in 1933, who sold it three years later to local business-man William McMullan. William had many business interests in the town, being owner of the gas works quay, the saltpans, a flax mill, a fleet of lorries, substantial property in High Street and warehouses in Meeting House Lane. He sub-let the spirit-grocers' to Miss Eileen Thompson and her mother, who applied for and obtained a licence for a hotel on the site.

Portaferry Hotel in the early days

John Herlilhy

The lease was eventually acquired by John Herlihy in 1980. John had considerable experience in the hospitality industry. He had previously managed the Russel Court Hotel on the Lisburn Road in Belfast. After only a month trading it was damaged in a bomb attack in September 1972 and was closed for repairs. It re-opened but was bombed again in 1976 and put out of business. In the same year John moved to the newly opened Everglades Hotel in Derry as its first General Manager and worked there until 1980.

In 1980 he purchased the Portaferry Hotel for himself and his wife to run as an independent hotel which he did very successfully for the next 25 years until his retirement in 2005. During his time, he extended and improved the hotel at every level, some still say that this period was the golden-age for the hotel. John would also go on to become President of the NI Hotels and Caterers Association.

In an article in the Belfast Telegraph on 31st October 2011 ostensibly about, Bill Wolsey's Beannchor Group taking over the hotel, there was more written about John Herlihy than the new owners:

"When John Herlihy owned it and ran it (with all the discipline of Josef Stalin and the charm of Bob Hope), the Portaferry Hotel was the destination to which time-poor people escaped from the stresses of life in Dublin and Belfast. It was here that they could kick their feet up in those 14 cosy bedrooms overlooking the swirling waters of the Lough and look out the window and wonder why they hadn't paid the fiver on the ferry to get over to Strangford, which looked even more compelling.

Strangford may be posher and slightly better spoken than Portaferry, but there's one thing it didn't have that Portaferry did: John Herlihy. This supremely well-educated and erudite man, always impeccably turned out and in complete command of all situations, introduced class to Portaferry and soon his hotel was the only reason why anybody visited. Until Ards Borough Council opened the aquarium.

Herlihy sold the hotel a few years ago and promptly moved next door with wife Marie; that way he could keep an eye on the monument he had built. This may explain why not a single pillow case, fork or dish was altered in any way during the tenure of the following owners."

While Strangford folk being posher than Portaferry may be something to discuss over dinner in the hotel, the comment about the aquarium proved significant. Undoubtedly, visitors to the Exploris Aquarium boosted business in the hotel which was only a short walk away. When it closed with uncertainty about funding for it to re-open again, it had a detrimental effect on the hotel, and when the workers turned up for work on Monday 19th October 2015, they found themselves locked out – the hotel had also closed. A business that had been in existence since before Edward Bryce's time was now in real danger of going under with considerable loss to the local economy.

A concerted campaign on both fronts, eventually, saw both premises re-opened and business again begin to pick up.

Portaferry Hotel present day

John Herlihy died on 25th September 2016, aged 76 years, living long enough to see the crisis averted and no doubt very satisfied to see the hotel back in the hands of local owners and continuing in business.

5 THE LIGHTSHIP MEN

Ted Edge   Henry Higginbotham   Eddie McMullan

In keeping with its maritime tradition Portaferry provided the Commissioners of Irish Lights with many lightship men. Ted Edge and Eddie McMullan are two of those that manned the South Rock Lightship over the years.

While James McCausland was in the business of getting ships off the rocks, it was the job of the lightship men, to warn shipping of their dangers and prevent them getting on in the first place. They were a special breed of men to whom a debt of gratitude is owed by many. Their wives also deserve a special mention, often having to bring up young families single-handedly, while their husbands were at sea.

South Rock Lightship

The South Rock Lightship got its name from the rocky outcrop just off Cloughy which was a danger to shipping. It was manned by up to seven of a crew, they had a large coal-fired stove for cooking and heating, but life on board was tough, there was always the danger of storms, being hit by passing ships and in war-time being a target for the enemy.

In 1950 the South Rock pulled her anchors and was in danger of grounding. The local life-boat stood by until it could get the crew off. It took patience, courage and resilience to live the life of a lightship man. Men passed their time in different ways, making and fitting model ships into bottles, was a traditional past-time and an art form in itself.

The South Rock was only automated in 1982 and was the last lightship around the coast of Ireland to be decommissioned on 25th February 2009. It had been there for just over 120 years. The actual ship had been replaced a few times, the last in service was the Light Vessel Gannet.

While lightships were targets during war-time the South Rock had survived two World Wars unscathed but, in the end, could not escape the march of progress. It was eventually replaced by a navigation buoy which cost about £300,000 whereas a ship would cost in the region of £5 million so in many ways the end was inevitable.

The Granuaile Irish Lights service vessel

On 25 February 2009 the South Rock was forlornly towed away behind the Irish Lights huge service vessel, the Granuaile, to await a new owner. One Irish Lights Commissioner commented 'although it was 55 years old it still only had delivery mileage,' but it was the end of an era, and a sad day for those who served on her for many years.

South Rock men - Ted in the fore-front and Eddie with coat over his arm

Ted Edge died on 15 July 2007, aged 81 years, and Eddie McMullan on 13th May 2009, aged 82 years. They were both well-known and respected lightship men, Henry Higginbotham from Wexford, was obviously less well-known. After almost 100 years his small headstone is showing signs of weathering but the following inscription can still be made out: -

IN
LOVING MEMORY OF
HENRY HIGGINBOTHAM
LATE OF WEXFORD
& CAPT S. R. LIGHTSHIP
DIED 5th MARCH 1921
AGED 57
RIP

Portaferry's proud tradition of providing lightship men was more than matched by Wexford. In fact, so many Wexford seamen served the Commissioners of Irish Lights that they were known as the 'Wexford Navy.'

Part of that 'Navy' was the Higginbotham family from Parnell Street in Wexford town. Henry's father was a lightship man, Henry and his five brothers worked for the Commissioners of Irish Lights, and Henry's own three sons also worked on the lightships. His brother Robert, unfortunately, lost his life at the age of 23 when the Puffin Lightship, off the coast of Cork, was swept away in a storm in 1896.

The Lucifer Shoals Lightship

The 1901 Census finds Henry working as a seaman on board the Lucifer Shoals Lightship in Wexford while his wife Bridget is at home with two young children. He is at home in Parnell Street for the 1911 Census with Bridget and six children, his occupation is recorded as "Mate in the Lightship Service."

Henry was subsequently promoted to Master of the South Rock Lightship but he was destined never to return to his native Wexford or to ever see his wife and family again. Sadly, he died on board the South Rock, after taking a heart attack, on 4th March 1921 and was buried in Ballyphilip Churchyard.

Someone still occasionally leaves flowers at his graveside, and for a man who spent his entire working life keeping a light shining to warn others of danger, it is fitting that a light still shines for him in Portaferry.

6 THE ENTERTAINERS

Joseph Tomelty

The Tomeltys' are rightly considered to be one of the most talented families ever to come out of Portaferry. A legacy of actors, writers, directors, musicians and singers continues down to the present generation.

Joseph Tomelty was born on 5th March 1911, the eldest of seven children living at 'the Shore' in Portaferry. His mother was Mary Drumgoole from Carrickmacross in County Monaghan and his father James Tomelty, a renown fiddle player.

Joseph left Ballyphilip Primary School at the age of 12 and was apprenticed to his father's trade as a house-painter and then moved to

Belfast to work as a painter in the Harland and Wolff Shipyard. Whilst in Belfast he attended Belfast Technical College where a Mr. Tipping, an English teacher, encouraged him to write.

From those humble beginnings he went on to star in film, television, radio and stage. His film roles include: Odd Man Out (1947), The Gentle Gunman (1952), Hobson's Choice (1954), Moby Dick (1956), A Night to Remember (1958 Titanic film) and many more.

Joseph Tomelty in The Gentle Gunman, 1952

He produced two novels Red is the Port Light (1948) and The Apprentice (1953), although he is probably better remembered as a playwright. His plays include: Barnum Was Right (1939), The End House (1944), All Souls' Night (1948), The Singing Bird (1948), and Is the Priest at Home (1954).

In 1948 he was commissioned by the BBC to write the weekly radio comedy series The

McCooeys. The series lasted seven years with a 6000-word script required for each episode. Jimmy Young starred as 'Derek the Window-Cleaner' which gave him the platform to go on to pursue his own comedy career.

Joseph was a founding member of the Ulster Group Theatre. In 1960 he starred alongside J. G. Devlin and Harry Towb in Sam Thompson's, highly controversial, 'Over the

Bridge' about a sectarian dispute in Harland and Wolff Shipyard which was directed by Jimmy Ellis.

Although the Bible states that 'no prophet is accepted in his home town' this was never the case with Joseph Tomelty. While some people who become famous tend to forget their roots, Joseph Tomelty got inspiration from his.

The Portaferry dialect is used in a great many of his plays, as are local names and place-names. The Gowlins, Gunn's Isle and Knockinelder Bay are all coastal references in All Souls' Night. Townlands Inishargie and Marlfield feature in the plays Idolatry in Inishargie and A Year in Marlfield. And the name "McCooeys" is probably a derivative from St. Cooey. It was once said by a local that, Joseph Tomelty was a very clever man, as he wrote down everything we said and then charged us to read it!

Portaferry is also renowned for its use of nicknames which often depict some characteristic of the person. In April in Assagh, the local postman is known as 'Stalin' for his pro-Communist and anti-cleric views; Tommy McFettridge, a local jazz musician, is known as 'Majesty'; and Jimmy has the nickname 'Drop O' Tay'. Local people could, therefore, easily relate to his plays and they were performed many times in St. Patrick's Parochial Hall, only a few hundred yards from where Joseph grew up.

His name lives on in Portaferry with a street named 'Joe Tomelty Drive' in his honour. A rafter in the old Bank Building at the corner of The Square also bears his name – Joseph autographed it while working there, painting the house, in the 1920s!

Joseph Tomelty died on 7th June 1995, the epitaph on his grave-stone is taken from All Souls' Night, when the ghost of Stephen appears to find his father kneeling down praying, and whispers: -

> "Pray for the dead that they may be loosed from their sins.
> Pray for the living that they may be loosed from their greed."

His two daughters, Roma and Frances, followed their father into film, television, and theatre. Roma has appeared in the films Miss Conception, Your Highness, Christmas Star and the TV series The Frankenstein Chronicles. Her first love though is theatre and she set up the Centre Stage company with her husband director Colin Carnegie, producing plays throughout Northern Ireland.

She appeared in the re-opening of the new Lyric Theatre in April 2011 in Arthur Millar's The Crucible. At the same venue later that year, to commemorate the centenary of her father's birth, she starred in All Souls' Night, as Katherine Quinn, a production and performance that was widely acclaimed. Frances was, likewise, talented and her film roles include: Bellman and True, Bullshot, Waking the Dead, and The Field. She has also appeared in a host of TV series such as

Bergerac, Inspector Morse, Mid-Summer Murders, Coronation Street and Cracker.

She was also a member of the Royal Shakespeare Company, with key roles in the Merchant of Venice, Richard III and A Midsummer's Night Dream. She also played Kate in the original production of Dancing at Lughnasa, at the Abbey Theatre, Dublin and featured in the opening of the Waterfront Hall in Belfast in 1997, alongside James Galway and Barry Douglas.

She is also probably known for her marriage to Gordon Sumner (aka Sting) with whom she had two children Joseph and Fuchsia, before divorcing in 1984. Both of her children, like their grandfather, are also in the entertainment business.

Peter Tomelty

Peter Tomelty, born in 1930, was the youngest brother of Joseph Tomelty. His talents came from the musical side of the family and while a sometime barber and barman, he was always a singer.

He had a classical Irish tenor voice and toured the world during his musical career. At just 16 years of age he was offered a job with the prestigious Carl Roma opera company but his family thought he was too young to leave home.

He got his big break on Ulster Television in the days of black and white TV and went on to make many appearances on 'The Half Door Club' television show. This provided the platform for him to become the host of the ever-popular television series on UTV, 'With a Fiddle and a Flute', which at the time was beating Coronation Street in the ratings.

He went on to have a very successful recording career with albums including The Irish Emigrant, Echoes of Ireland, The Mountains of Mourne and Lovely Derry on the Banks of the Foyle.

Aristotle and Jackie Onassis at Harland and Wolff, 1970

He performed in concerts around the world. Memorably he performed for Aristotle and Jackie Onassis when they visited Harland and Wolff Shipyard in 1970. Aristotle Onassis was a Greek shipping magnate, one of the richest men in the world at the time, and had part ownership in Harland and Wolff.

When he retired from the music scene he ran the popular bar, 'Peter Tomelty's In…,' at the corner of The Square and Church Street. He was, however, persuaded out of retirement by his niece Roma to perform in the musical Moore's Irish Melodies, which was a huge success in Britain and Ireland.

Peter married comedienne and dancer Gertie Wine who went on to run a very successful dance school in Portaferry for many years.

He died on 23rd January 2007, aged 76 years, leaving a legacy of musical memories that can still be enjoyed today.

Rosemary Woods

Rosemary Woods was a very talented singer/songwriter with a huge following in Ireland, Scotland, Wales, Germany and America. After the success of her debut album, 'Irish Ballads', she went on to make 'Walking Together', which proved to be even more popular.

Rosemary Woods and Siobhan Skates

She teamed up with Australian singer/ songwriter Siobhan Skates to produce 'Walking It Alone Together' which captured the unique blend of their harmonies. They featured on "Anderson on the Road' TV show playing "Papa's on the Rooftop' at the ferry terminal in Portaferry.

In September 2010 Rosemary appeared at the Four Seasons of Peace Concert at the Helix in Dublin, for the UN International Day of Peace. She sang the self-penned 'Talk to Me', poignantly touching on our own troubles and search for peace.

Sadly, Rosemary died on 29th September 2019 and a celebration concert was held in her honour in St. Patrick's Community Centre. It was hosted by her friends, The Sands Family, and featured Kieran Goss and Anne Kinsella, Briege Murphy, Siobhan Skates and Mathew Fleming, and raised more than £9,000 for Marie Curie Cancer Care.

Liam Gilmore

Although not achieving the international acclaim of the aforementioned performers, no mention of Portaferry entertainers would be complete without reference to Liam Gilmore.

Liam was a natural comic and actor and was at the heart of every concert, play, pantomime or show of any description in Portaferry for decades. He was a proponent of amateur dramatics, before that term was even thought of, and appeared in many of the Joseph Tomelty plays performed in St. Patrick's Hall.

Liam, centre-backrow, with other Portaferry Gala committee members and guests

He had an innate sense of what entertained and made people laugh. Unsurprisingly, he was a founding member of Portaferry Gala Week in July 1967, which has been held every year since its inception and is now the longest running festival week in Ireland. The format that Liam helped devise is still very much the backbone of the festival to the present day. Liam Gilmore died on 1st September 2016 at the grand age of 90, a life well lived.

7 THE TROUBLES

Father Hugh Mullan

Father Hugh Mullan was a local Portaferry priest. He was the Master of Ceremonies when St. Patrick's Church celebrated its bi-centenary in 1962. The dignified and simple inscription on his gravestone: "Died serving his people in Ballymurphy," belies a tragic event from our troubled past.

'The Troubles' in Northern Ireland began in 1969 and continued up to the signing of the Belfast Good Friday Agreement in 1998. During that period more than 3,000 people were killed and thousands more seriously injured.

With the Troubles spiraling out of control the Northern Ireland Prime Minister, Brian Faulkner, and the UK Prime Minister, Edward Heath, agreed to the introduction of internment without trial, in 1971.

A list of 450 people suspected of being in the IRA was drawn up and 342 were arrested and interned by the British Army under Operation Demetrius. All those arrested were Irish Nationalists, many not being involved at all with the IRA and many who were had managed to avoid arrest.

This operation led to the worse riots that Northern Ireland had ever seen. Hundreds of vehicles were hijacked and burned, factories and buildings were set on fire, and barricades were erected to keep the army out.

Between the 9th and 11th August, 24 people had been killed, 20 civilians, 2 members of the IRA, and 2 British Army personnel. Of the 20 civilians who had died, 17 were killed by the British Army and 3 by unknown assailants.

At the time Father Mullan was serving in Corpus Christi parish in West Belfast's, Ballymurphy, where 11 Catholic civilians were killed by the 1st Battalion, Parachute Regiment, in an event that became known as the Ballymurphy Massacre.

Prior to the outbreak of rioting, Father Mullan had been striving to secure some protection from the authorities for his parishioners, but to no avail. When he heard that Bobby Clarke had been shot in Springfield Park, he rang the nearby Henry Taggart Army base, to explain that he was going to the aid of the injured man.

He ventured out waving a white cloth and managed to reach Bobby Clarke to administer the Last Rites, but on leaving the field he was shot in the back. Harrowing eye-witness accounts recall that Father Mullan could be heard praying in both English and Latin as he lay dying for some time after being shot.

A tribute to Father Mullan, from an unlikely source, emerged during the inquest into the Ballymurphy Massacre in October 2019. The following letter from Lieutenant Colonel Peter Chiswell, the officer commanding the 3rd Battalion, Parachute Regiment, sent to Bishop William Philbin was read out at the hearing: -

FROM LIEUTENANT COLONEL P J CROSSELL MBE

3RD BATTALION THE PARACHUTE REGIMENT

British Forces Post Office 617

The Right Reverend William Philbin, DD
"Lisbreen"
Somerton Road
BELFAST

19th August 1971

My Lord Bishop,

Because my Battalion is on an exercise in a remote part of Ghana we did not learn of the terrible and tragic death of Father Hugh Mullan until yesterday.

I write to you now with a deep sense of sorrow and loss, to express the sympathies of every officer and parachute soldier in the 3rd Battalion, The Parachute Regiment.

We knew this fine Christian man, Father Hugh Mullan very well during our four and a half months on peace keeping duties in SW Belfast. In the face of the most appalling troubles, we found in him a priest to whom we could go for help, advice, guidance and encouragement. His charm, commonsense and total dedication to his Parish soon won our respect. Later, as we worked together, a bond of friendship developed between us which meant so much to us all, particularly to those officers and Senior NCO's who had daily contact with him.

I humbly submit My Lord Bishop, that if ever we have seen a true example of Christian courage then we have been privileged to see it in the work and ministry of Father Hugh Mullan.

I ask you to accept from us all our deepest and most profound sympathies on the loss of this outstanding priest, and I would like you to know that sharing your own sorrow are some 500 parachute soldiers of 3 PARA.

Yours sincerely,

Peter Crissell

As his gravestone states, Father Mullan died serving his people in Ballymurphy, on the first day of internment on the 9th August 1971. He was buried at the front of St. Patrick's Chapel in one of the largest funerals ever seen in the parish.

Christopher Byers

While the Troubles continued to rage throughout Northern Ireland, Portaferry got on with life and with each other, much as it had always done. This peace was shattered on 5th March 1974.

At about 9.20pm that evening, a cream-coloured Morris 1100 with a 200-pound bomb on board was driven up to the International Bar at the corner of The Square and Church Street. Two men jumped out and made their getaway in another car which was later found burnt out at Tullycross, about three miles away.

Five minutes later a warning was telephoned to Portaferry Police Station. The two constables on duty had only twelve minutes to evacuate the densely populated area before the bomb exploded. The blast almost completely demolished the building and wrecked houses within a 50-yard radius. Local residents took refuge in their back-gardens, and thanks to the speedy reaction of the police only two people received minor injuries.

International Bar after bomb explosion, 1974

The structural damage to the building was so severe that, for safety reasons, work on its demolition began almost immediately. So too did its re-building and the bar was soon back in business as a key place of entertainment in the town. But the bombers were to strike again, this time with a no-warning bomb when the bar was full of people, on 5th June 1976. The Down Recorder report on 8th June captures the grim consequences: -

HUNT IS ON FOR PORTAFERRY BOMBERS

"Police are still hunting the killers of the 22 year-old Portaferry youth who died in Saturday night's explosion in the village.

Christopher Byers, of Cloughey Road, Portaferry, was among a packed crowd at the International Bar when the killers left a 20 Ib. bomb shortly after 11pm. It exploded without warning in a small alley at the rear of the buildings.

The dead youth was apparently caught in the worst part of the building as the roof collapsed and rubble fell everywhere. He died almost immediately.

Ambulances raced to the scene from Newtownards hospital as rescuers formed a chain to bring the injured out from the debris. Dozens of people were injured, at least two of them seriously.

It was a strange explosion which devastated one building but left others in the small narrow street virtually unscathed. It was in the same street where Portaferry suffered its first bomb attack 18 months ago.

The International Bar literally crumpled like a stack of cards and as one local put it: "It's dead lucky that at least 50 weren't killed. It's a miracle that anyone walked out of that."

In the early light of Sunday morning, as locals made their way to church services to pray for the dead and injured, the full extent of the damage was seen in stark reality. A building reduced to half its size could well have been a death-pit for many.

The International Bar, first bombed in February (sic) 1974, was one of Portaferry's most popular bars. Just as it was every Saturday night it was packed with people enjoying the usual sing-song to a local band.

The band's instruments lay pitifully in the remains long after the injured were ferried off to hospital. Two members of the group were among the more seriously injured. The entire top floor ceiling fell heavily towards the end of the bar where the band's small platform was situated.

A maroon Maxi was seen speeding off from the scene minutes after the explosion but although all roads were quickly sealed off the bombers escaped.

The explosion numbed the small Portaferry community and tempers ran high throughout the night. A group of plain clothes Army personnel who parked near the scene were forced to produce identification by several locals alerted by the earlier incident.

Condemning the bombing, South Down constituency representative, Mr. Paddy O'Donoghue, said it was another incident in the organised campaign against Catholic life and property in the North Down area.

Mr. O'Donoghue said: "It is clear from this and previous incidents in Kircubbin, Bangor and Ballycran that the minority in the Ards peninsula is under threat from a Loyalist cell.

"The law-abiding community must reject these men of violence and co-operate in the task of bringing them to justice," he added."

Seat in graveyard in memory of Christopher Byers

The Bar was never re-built and the building lay derelict for nearly forty years. The above seat in the graveyard donated by the Byers family, in memory of Christopher, is a sad reminder of our troubled past and senseless loss of life.

8 FOOTBALL'S FOUNDING FATHERS

Portaferry United League and Cup Winners 1920

Portaferry has always had a strong footballing tradition. This photograph was taken 100 years ago to celebrate Portaferry United becoming the first team to win the Ards Summer League and the inaugural Ards Challenge Cup in 1920. It was less than two years after the First World War had ended and life and sport were returning to normal. Eight teams entered the league that year, although not all were able to fulfill all their fixtures, the final league placings were as follows: -

	P	W	L	D	F	A	Pts
Portaferry Un.	14	11	1	2	37	9	24
Portavogie Olp.	14	9	2	3	25	4	21
B'halbert Amat.	13	8	4	2	13	14	18
Allen Swifts	14	8	4	2	26	17	18
Granshaw Un.	12	6	5	3	12	14	15
Warren Swifts	13	2	10	2	10	25	6
Roddens Albion	13	2	12	0	3	30	4
Abbey Rangers	14	1	12	1	7	19	3

Ards Summer League 1920

Ten teams entered the Cup competition with the above teams being joined by another Portavogie side and Ballygalget. Portavogie Olympic again lost out to Portaferry in the final.

The reward for winning the league and cup double was a day trip to Bangor. Some 60 members of the club boarded two Ards Transport Motor char-a- bancs at 9.00 am in The Square, on 16th September 1920, to commence the journey. On reaching Bangor they "partook of a sumptuous repast, served in excellent style," in the Downshire Hotel. After the meal Mr. Wm. Bryce, chairman of the league, presented the players with their gold medals, thereafter, the players and club officials called at Lyttle's Photographic Studio in Bangor, where the above photograph was taken.

As is often the case success breeds success and we find the following report in the Newtownards Chronicle and County Down Observer, on 12th March 1921: -

Ards Summer Football League

"Football enthusiasts residing in Quinton district are taking time by the fore-lock, and their first meeting has been held for the purpose of inaugurating a club to take part in games of this organisation. The meeting was held at Ballycam, and the chair was occupied by Mr. Jim Moran, a veteran organiser in football circles. It was decided to name the club "The Ards Celtic." The following were elected office-bearers for the season : - President, Mr. T. H. Lynch; vice-presidents, Messrs. J. H. Crangle and H. D. Lennon; treasurer, Mr. H. J. Conway; secretary, Mr. Jim Moran. These gentlemen, with the assistance of a duly elected committee, were entrusted with the important work of securing suitable grounds, and also to draw up a code of rules for the guidance of the club."

This is possibly the inaugural meeting of a team that was to become Ballycam Celtic (Ballycam being a townland just outside Portaferry) and would lead to the establishment of two teams in the town. If so, this team remained in existence for a long time and at the helm for many of those years was Tom Kelly.

Tom Kelly

Tom managed Ballycam Celtic for decades and was something of an iconic figure on the sideline. He was a football man through and through with great motivational skills and many young players have him to thank for their debuts and chance to progress into senior football.

Ballycam Celtic Ards Summer League Cup Winners

It was a well-run club that had many successes over the years. The above team, Tom extreme right back-row, having beaten Portavogie Albion in the Lower Ards knock-out cup. In 1976 Tom was elected Chairman of the Down Area League and the Tom Kelly KO Cup was introduced. He died on 20th January 2006, aged 81 years, having made a significant contribution to local football.

Nicky McMullan and Rennie McMullan

In the late 1960s a group of men in the town started a Celtic Supporters Club and they ran a small youth-club from premises in Ferry Street. An offshoot of the Club was the formation of a youth team, Celtic Boys. The coaches of this team were, Nicholas (Nicky) and Lorenzo (Rennie) McMullan, both gifted amateur footballers. Rennie had played for Shorts in the Amateur League and went on to play for Ards FC in the Irish League.

Celtic Boys 1968

Nicky and Rennie are pictured, extreme left and right respectively, in the previous photograph taken in the Club's headquarters in Ferry Street. The team competed in the Ards Schoolboy League and Nicky and Rennie were responsible for producing the original 'Invincibles'. The team never lost a game and won everything before them. Unfortunately, Nicky and Rennie both died young at the ages of 52 and 47 respectively.

Tom McGrattan   Seamus McMullan   Davy Fitzsimmons

By the mid-1970s youth football in the town had again ceased although the enthusiasm for football had not. Most evenings the football-field was packed with young boys playing football. There was no limit to the number in each team, and no time-keeping either, as the match finished whenever it was too dark to continue.

Four men who closely watched these proceedings were Billy Fitzsimmons (not buried at Ballyphilip), Davy Fitzsimmons, Tom McGrattan and Seamus McMullan. They could see the potential of these young players and decided to form a youth team. The team was named Burn Brae Rovers after the street leading to the pitch. The first Committee was Manager/Chairman – Billy Fitsimmons, Trainer/Vice Chairman – Tom McGrattan, Secretary/Assistant Trainer – Davy Fitzsimmons and Treasurer – Seamus McMullan.

The team was entered into the Downpatrick Youth Football League in 1973. This League had settled into a somewhat cosy arrangement whereby the same two teams usually shared the spoils each year. But the 'noisy neighbours' had arrived and Burn Brae had no respect for reputations. They narrowly missed out on the league title in their first year and won the League Cup, beating all the best teams in the league.

Burn Brae Rovers 1975

In the above photograph Davy Fitzsimmons is pictured front-row extreme left with Tom McGrattan beside him in the back-row, Billy Fitsimmons and Seamus McMullan are extreme right back-row. With only a couple of additions to the squad, the same group of lads who had entered the Downpatrick Youth Football League stepped up to senior football, firstly in the newly formed Down Area League in the 1974/75 season, and then the Newcastle and District League Division B the following year. Tom McGrattan took over as manager, a post he held for many years and deserves particular mention for his hard-work and dedication. An inspired signing of Tom's was local PE teacher Sean McGourty, as the report in the Down Recorder on 20 January 1976 confirms:-

"Soccer – Sean McGourty, the 25 year-old Portaferry school teacher – in only his first season in Newcastle league football – finds himself well clear of his rivals in the Down Recorder's leading goal scorers' competition. The prolific Burn Brae Rovers striker has rattled in 26 league goals, including five hat-tricks in 19 games, to put his side in a challenging position in the league's Division B in their first season."

The Rovers finished top scorers in the league, gained promotion from Division B in their first season, but missed out on the title to Saintfield United. Portaferry now had another good team, and when Portaferry Celtic and Burn Brae Rovers amalgamated to form Portaferry Rovers FC they had one very good team, which went from strength to strength.

The Rovers win their first County Antrim Shield 1999/2000

Portaferry Rovers can look back at a prolonged period of success, they won every honour in the Newcastle League, two County Antrim Shields, and after being accepted into the Northern Amateur Football League, successive promotions from Division 2C to Division 2A, and now play intermediate football in Division 1B, competing in such prestigious competitions as the Steel and Sons Cup and the Irish Cup.

They can, perhaps, also look back at a long journey that began more than 100 years ago, and to the founding fathers who kept football alive in the town through hard-work, commitment and enthusiasm, as the foundation for their success.

Frank Blair

Frank Blair was a well-known Portaferry character, although in keeping with his generation who had a close affiliation with their townlands, he always insisted that he was from Ballymartyr, a townland near Knockinelder, rather than Portaferry itself. He was a familiar figure cycling the three miles in and out of town on his vintage black bike, until he moved into town, in the later years of his life.

Frank could easily have slotted into 'The Entertainers' section of this book as he was Liam Gilmore's go-to-man for a comic-turn in any local concert. It is unclear if Liam directed Frank or simply 'egged-him-on' but he was sure to bring the house down with whatever role he was given.

But surprisingly Frank finds himself in the football pages and perhaps, even more surprisingly, as the first Portaferry man to have played football at Wembley Stadium!

The original Wembley Stadium, was initially known as the Empire Stadium, as it was constructed to house the Empire Exhibition. It opened in 1923 after it was built in exactly 300 days at a cost of £750,000. It hosted the FA Cup Final between Bolton Wanderers and West Ham just four days after the building work had been completed.

This became known as the White Horse Final as mounted police were needed to control an estimated crowd of 300,000 spectators in a stadium with a capacity of 125,000. In the end, with the spectators packed around the side-lines, the Wanderers went on to win the first Wembley final 2–0. From this inauspicious beginning Wembley would go on to host every FA Cup Final up to the year 2000, as well as seven European Cup Finals, the 1948 Olympics and the 1966 World Cup Final.

Building of Wembley Stadium, 1923

Frank was born on 6th November 1901 and as a young man in his twenties left Portaferry to seek work in London. As the above photograph shows there was plenty of work to be had building Wembley Stadium and Frank was taken on. It is not known if it was because of or in spite of Frank's contribution that the remarkable feat of building Wembley in 300 days was achieved. As the building work was being finalised, the pitch was also being laid, the final having already been scheduled to be played there.

And what do young men in their twenties with a big pitch and a football do during their lunch-break? They play football of course! Apparently, they were permitted to do so to help the newly-laid pitch settle, in advance of the final in a few days' time. And so, along with some of his co-workers, Frank ran out onto the hallowed turf of Wembley to become the first man from Portaferry to play football at Wembley Stadium in 1923.

Frank returned to Ballymartyr to marry Bridget Kennedy at Ballyphilip Church on 30th April 1938. He settled into married life and worked locally, his brief sporting career had come to an end, but not to be forgotten.

8 PRECIOUS TIME

Elizabeth Mahon

In 'The Secret Diary of Adrian Mole Aged 13¾' the author, Sue Townsend, depicts how young people can be very precise about their age. There is no reason why we should not continue to do so as we get older, perhaps, there is even more reason to count every day and make every day count. For whatever reason, this headstone proudly records that Elizabeth Mahon died on the 18th August 1994 having lived to the grand age of 86¾.

'Digging Up The Past' uncovers a rich history of those who made their time count and who are still remembered as a result. The parish priests who built up the parish from little more than a mud-walled mass house nearly 260 years ago. The brave mariners who answered the call of the sea and sometimes paid with their lives. The men who established pubs, a hotel, cinema and dance-hall for our recreation. From lightships to an air-ambulance and the men who spent their lives helping others. The entertainers, always remembered through their work, which lives on. Those who were, unfortunately, in the wrong place at the wrong time during the Troubles and departed at a young age. The football men with a history stretching back over 100 years. The men who went to war and never returned, the first Portaferry man to die in World War I and the first Portaferry man to play football at Wembley Stadium.

For all those interred in Ballyphilip Churchyard and, particularly, those mentioned above may they Rest In Peace.

For those reading this book, an Irish Blessing: -

"May you be in Heaven a full half-hour before the Devil knows you are dead."

ABOUT THE AUTHOR

J B McMullan is a taphophile from Portaferry. Author also of Us Boys In Portaferry.

Printed in Great Britain
by Amazon